Losing North

Losing North

Musings on Land, Tongue and Self

Nancy Huston

McArthur & Company
Toronto

Published in Canada in 2002 by McArthur & Company

McArthur & Company
322 King Street West, Suite 402
Toronto, Ontario
M5V 1J2

National Library of Canada Cataloguing in Publication

    Huston, Nancy, 1953-

    Losing north: musings on land, tongue and self / Nancy Huston.

    Translation of: Nord perdu
    ISBN 1-55278-315-4

    Huston, Nancy, 1953-. 2. Huston, Nancy, 1953—
    Views on expatriation. I. Title.

    PS8565.U8255Z53 2002   C843'.54   C2002-903348-9
    PQ3919.2.H87Z47 2002

Composition / Jacket design & f/x: *Mad Dog Design*

Printed in Canada by *Transcontinental Printing Inc.*

The publisher would like to acknowledge the financial support of the Government of Canada through the Book Publishing Industry Development Program (BPIDP) and the Canada Council for our publishing activities. The publisher further wishes to acknowledge the financial support of the Ontario Arts Council for our publishing program.

10 9 8 7 6 5 4 3 2 1

For Lorne,
tongue, soul and blood brother

Home is where you start from.

– T.S. Eliot, *East Coker*

Contents

My own heart let me have more pity on; let
Me live to my sad self hereafter kind,
Charitable; not live this tormented mind
With this tormented mind tormenting yet.

– Gerard Manley Hopkins

Take-Off

"I do not like myself. Yes." The words of Sviatoslav Richter.

To begin with, self-hatred. For whatever reason.

All sorts of behaviour can be inspired by self-hatred. You can become an artist. Commit suicide. Adopt a new name, a new country, a new language.

All of the above (Romain Gary).

Orientation

To be disorientated is to lose the east.

In French, "losing north" means forgetting what you were going to say. *Losing track of what's going on. Losing your marbles.* It is something you should avoid at all costs. Something that's always spoken of negatively, to say that one hasn't done it. "My, he certainly doesn't lose the north, does he?" is the way the expression is used. Never "Ah, too bad – he's lost the north."

To be all abroad is what my excellent French-English dictionary suggests by way of translation. An expression which, taken literally, means to be in a foreign country. But if, in turn, you take the English-French dictionary and look up the expression *To be all abroad,* what you find is *to be scattered every which way,* or *to the four winds, to talk twaddle, to be off one's rocker* – which is not at all the same thing!

Dictionaries confuse us, they lead us astray, they plunge us into that frightening magma *between languages,* in which words lose their meanings, refuse to mean, start out meaning one thing and end up meaning quite another.

The North is what I intended to say.

What I should have said. Theoretically. What I was supposed to say, in the event that I had something to say.

The North is where I hail from. In referring to it, the French invariably specify that it is "great," even rigging it out with a capital letter. No one ever says, speaking of me: she comes from the small North. Always the Great. In the French imagination, its hugeness makes up for its emptiness. The Great North is enormous but contains nothing. "Acres of snow," as Voltaire famously put it. Millions of square miles of ice. People find it admirable but have no idea what to say about it, or even how to question you about it. They know that it's cold out there. ("God it's cold!" Thirty years after leaving Canada, I insist on being allowed to pronounce this sentence in Paris, and to be cold in Paris, damn it, without having to hear, "But you're from Canada, you must be used to it!" – a comment which reduces me to my country of origin, even if it doesn't pack me off there like an illegal immigrant.)

"The North," in this case, is also a figure of speech. The truth is that the latitude of Calgary, my native city, is roughly the same as that of Paris, my adopted city. "The North" is an *image*, indicating cold weather and sparse population.

Be this as it may, "the True North, Strong and Free" is where I hail from; it's even part of my national anthem.

"True North," as everyone knows, is the actual, geographical North, not the one indicated by the compass – not the North Pole. In French, "to lose your compass" means to lose your head, to be "completely lost or disorientated."

Your head, in other words, is what points you north.

And you mustn't ever lose these things. Your head. The north.

You mustn't panic. So let's not panic.

Let's try to get our bearings.

"Strong and free" is straightforward enough. I can translate it into French with no difficulty whatsoever: *fort et libre.* There's no possible ambiguity. Either you're strong and free or you're not, right? France's national anthem tells how the nation's furrows have been nourished with blood, so in all likelihood France is strong and free as well. What about *your* country – is it strong and free, too? What's it called? Oh, really? And since when? Mine's been called Canada for a mere two centuries. Before that, it didn't have a name; it didn't exist. What about yours? And who are your ancestors? Are you filled with patriotic ardour? No, this is not a survey; I'm just trying to figure out what's what here. Are you proud to come from the country you come from? Why? What have you done to deserve it? And what would "betraying" your country mean to you? Leaving it? Abandoning it forever? Making love to another country?

My country was the North, the Great North, the True North Strong and Free.

I betrayed it, and I've lost it.

This fall marks the twenty-fifth anniversary of my arrival in France. I settled here in 1973 and, as I write these words, it is 1998. A quarter of a century has gone by (yes, *time passes*, that's what I was trying to get across a moment ago – everything is relative, the age of a country, the age of an individual, these things don't exist in the absolute because all you have to do is wait and time will pass, turning young people into old people and young countries into old countries, whether they like it or not) – more than half my life. If I'd been born in 1973, I'd be an adult already, a woman of twenty-five. I was *not* born in 1973, however – ah, that's where the shoe pinches – and it's not *at all* the same thing to have lived in a country for the first twenty-five or another twenty-five years of one's life.

The North – the Great North – left its indelible imprint upon me.

What kind of imprint is it? What does it look like? In what ways have I remained the child of my native land? *In all ways* . . . for the simple reason that I spent my childhood there, and that nothing in the world resembles childhood. Popular wisdom notwithstanding, you only get one of them; even Alzheimer's can't give you a second one.

Thus, though I've been living in France much longer than my own children (ha ha, that's obvious), I'll never be as French as they are. It's a bit like equality – everyone in the family is French, but some of us are more French than others. (Thanks to the relatively low amount of melanin in the pigmentation of their skin, the French-born offspring of a Canadian female and a Bulgarian male find it easy to be French. The French-born offspring of a Nigerian female and a Cambodian male would have a much more difficult time of it.)

"Do you feel French now?" people often ask me. (To live abroad is to be perpetually subjected to silly questions.)

What on earth might it be like to "feel French"? How would I know, were it to happen to me one day?

Foreigners can be given French nationality (the verb "to naturalize" in French also designates what taxidermists do to dead animals); they can be given French diplomas and French honours, they can even be elected to the glorious French Academy and cherish dreams of French immortality . . . They will never be French for all that, because no one has the power to give them a French childhood.

So the answer is: no.

(Even *with* a French childhood, there are any number of people who have a hard time feeling French! Without one, it's impossible.)

Your childhood stays with you all your life, no matter where you go.

A few weeks ago, I was invited to an evening of discussion and debate about my work in a library in the suburbs. The husband of one of the librarians was sent to pick me up in Paris and drive me there. I rapidly gathered that the man had been forced to read my books against his will, and was eager to take advantage of this hour alone with me in the car to express his resentment. Between conversations on his cellphone, he told me in no uncertain terms that my novels left him cold.

"Abortion and infanticide," he said. "I mean, you've got to admit that those are basically women's themes."

"I can see that you might not feel concerned as a man," I said, nodding. "But as children, we're all concerned, don't you think?"

"Ha!" The man let out a rather nasty laugh. "I doubt that there are many children among your readers."

"No, no," I hastened to say, "I mean *you*, as a child."

"But I'm not a child!" he objected.

"But of course you are! We're all our ages at once, aren't we? Childhood is like the stone at the heart of the fruit – the fruit doesn't become hollow as it grows! The flesh may swell and ripen and soften around it, but that doesn't make the stone disappear."

"And I suppose," said my driver, now fairly seething with rage, "that there is no disagreement allowed."

Poor guy, who was nothing but an adult. (When I say poor, I mean voluntarily impoverished.) *He* wasn't in exile, that's for sure.

People in exile are rich – rich with the accumulated sum of their contradictory identities.

The truth is that all of us have multiple identities – if only because all of us were children once, then teenagers, and are these things no longer, yet are them still.

Allow me to formulate here, for the first time, a

hypothesis to which I shall return time and again in the course of this essay – so often, in fact, that it could qualify as the essay's *leitmotiv*, its main theme, or even (God forbid) its MESSAGE, so I may as well go the whole hog and put it in italics: *Expatriates are consciously (and often painfully) aware of a number of truths which, unbeknownst to others, shape the human condition in general.* One of these truths is the absolutely unique nature of childhood, and the fact that it never leaves you. No expatriate can be oblivious to this fact, whereas it's quite possible for impatriates to go through life with the reassuring illusion of continuity and self-evidence.

Disorientation

To be in geographic exile is to be split in two chronologically: the place where you spent your childhood is far away; there's a radical break between then and now.

You've got one life *here*, and another *there* – with everything the word *life* implies: codes deciphered and mastered; systems of reference learned; the incredible complexity of the everyday; possibly even a different language, which is a whole world unto itself (a theme we'll come back to later). Even if you haven't adopted a new idiom, you've learned the ins and outs of a new political system, new ways of cooking and eating, new manners, customs, slangwords, a new History, new stories, a new literary tradition, and so on and so forth.

Here, you set aside what you used to be. The people around you haven't the vaguest notion of your childhood, with its nursery rhymes, food, schools, friends, neighbourhoods – and it's not worth the effort, you don't want to bore them by giving them a crash course on Western Canada, Protestantism, wheat fields, country and western music, oil derricks, freight trains, piano lessons, pic- nics, mountain lakes, your father, your mother, everything that shaped you, contributed to making you who you are, they know nothing of any of this and you tell yourself that it doesn't really matter because you're convinced that you preserve it all inside of you somewhere, deep within your heart – or your memory – and that, even if you never talk about it, you can never lose it.

There, you set aside what you've become. Yes – the folks back home take little interest in the things you've been thinking, saying, reading, seeing and doing, day after day for decades. It's too complicat- ed, it's not worth the effort, you don't want to give them a crash course on Chirac, Mitterrand, Duras, the Place des Vosges at dawn, your bakery, your pub- lisher, your favourite radio station, your friends, your neighbours in the region of Berry, it would be tedious – and besides, you wouldn't know where to start! So you keep mum, you grin, you talk to them silent about Bill Clinton and Philip Roth, the Fine Arts Museum and the Boston Harbor, the heat wave in Florida and the televangelists, and so on and so forth. Why not? You know about those things, too, more or less, and when you don't know you can always listen. It never hurts to listen.

That's what exile is about. Mutilation. Guilt. Self-censorship.

You communicate with others using either the child or the adult part of yourself. Never both.

In this case, however, the little refrain I worked out earlier does not apply. On the contrary. In this case, the joke is at the expense of the expatriates, and it takes them a while to catch on. Truths which are perfectly obvious to most people are discovered by them in shocked disbelief.

As a general rule – at least in our day and age in the modern Western world – impatriates find it natural to break free of their origins, the values they absorbed in their youth. They're not in the least surprised when, upon reaching middle age, they look back and see the gulf that separates them from their parents.

Why are we expatriates so taken aback? It's because we're accustomed to seeing the differences between *them* and *us*, between yesterday and today, as an effect of our exile, our change of countries. In our minds, the abyss was neither more nor less than an expanse of ocean measuring 31,800,000 square miles.

This time, though, the impatriates are right.

I'm reminded of *The Square* and other early writings of Annie Ernaux, with their poignant descriptions of her progressive estrangement from her parents' social milieu. "This was the time," writes Ernaux, "when everything that was closest to me seemed foreign"; "The universe was topsy-turvy"; "I felt cut off from myself . . ."

Reading the novel manuscript of a friend from Victoria the other day, I was brought up short by a passage that described the same uncomfortable sense of division:

> [Delaney]...did not know how to place himself comfortably in the environment of his growing up. He did not know how to visit what was once his home. One can never visit home. There were parts of himself he had left behind not because he wanted to let go of them but because he did not know how to take them with him. Going back to the house and seeing the marsh was like seeing a small, destitute child reach out his hand to him, palm upwards. He did not know how to respond, he did not know what the child wanted . . .

And then the process would fold back on

itself and he would return to the university to find the parts of himself he could not take with him to the marsh.

Matthew Manera, *A Turning of Leaves*

To be in social exile is to be ontologically divided in two. Each part of your being is a world unto itself, and the two worlds are not only dissimilar but hostile and hierarchized. There are virtually no points of intersection between them, and *you* are one of these points. Like Delaney, like Annie Ernaux, you keep going back and forth between the two worlds, and it makes you miserable.

But one form of exile can conceal another. For years, a social split can be concealed by a geographical one. You explain away all the misunderstandings between you and your family by thinking of them as the result of the culture gap – the difficulty of understanding one society in the vocabulary of the other. The truth, however, is that your soul, like your body, has moved away from its point of departure. And the day comes when you're forced to recognize that you no longer share the values of the people who brought you into the world, talked and sang to you as a child, cuddled and fed you in the warmth and comfort of the family home. Even if you haven't been initiated into the intricacies of a foreign language, you no longer speak their tongue.

Until very recently, I hadn't fully realized that my own exile was *also* social; in other words, that it reflected not only the difference between Europe and North America, but a difference between two spiritual environments, two ways of looking at the world . . .

Last July, I spent ten days near my father and stepmother's house in New Hampshire, delighted at the chance to get reacquainted with the multitudinous Huston tribe, including in-laws and grandchildren. And for ten long days, I lived a large and luscious lie – namely, that I was not forty-five but fifteen years old. Numerous circumstances converged to encourage and condone this lie. The weather, first of all, because when we left Alberta in 1968 to come and settle in New England, it was summertime, too. There was the same bright sunlight, the same purity of air and water, the same generous beauty of the forest – a breathtaking mixture of maple, pine and birch . . . Thirty years had passed, but my bucolic high school was still there, nestled at the heart of the woods, and the long-haired students lounging on its front steps could have been the self-same hippies of my class of '70 . . . The signs that flashed past us at the side of the road hadn't changed either – "Corn for sale," "State Park," "Apples, Cider, Maple Syrup," "Protect Our Children" . . . My parents had just moved back to the house they'd lived in from 1974 to 1988, and I felt a giddying sense of familiarity as I moved about in the kitchen, opening drawers and finding silver-ware, playing-cards, safety matches – everything in its place . . . From dawn to dusk, as we all threw our-selves into the task of refurbishing the house, the radio played Golden Oldies – *Mister Postman, Hey Jude, Take a Walk on the Wild Side* . . . hits from the sixties whose words rose naturally to my lips. True, my husband and son were there to remind me that I was no longer a nymphet – but everything was so relaxed and laid-back that we were somehow freed from our habitual roles – dressed in shorts, T-shirts and bathing-suits, weightless, neutral, moving about in an atmosphere of unreality.

Thus, in the company of my older and younger relatives, I swam in the very lakes I'd swum in thirty years before; with my father at my side, I drove down the backroads on which I'd learned to drive at age seventeen with my father at my side; and the campfire over which we roasted our hotdogs, ham-burgers and vegetable shish-kebabs in the nearby State Park was identical to the campfires of my youth. Moreover, I had no trouble taking part in the family conversation – everything was easy, familiar, recognizable . . .

Easy, yes, on one condition: that I forget about the fact that for the past quarter of a century I'd been living on the far side of the Atlantic Ocean, speaking a foreign language and writings books in that language.

Oh, yes, it was easy . . .

And traumatic.

Because, when you come right down to it, if your own family knows next to nothing about your life – its shape, context, passions and preoccupations, hopes and ambitions – perhaps your life isn't as interesting as you thought it was.

Go ahead. Try and describe it to us. We're listening. Uh-huh . . . What's so extraordinarily fascinating about *that?* Ah . . . ? Never heard of it. Never heard of her, him, them. Nope. Don't know what you're talking about.

What is important?

Do you see what I mean? You're beginning to lose the north.

Even if you wrote to them less and less frequently as the years went by, your friends and relatives from "back home" were always present in your mind as the witnesses of your life abroad. Year after year, you described and explained to them precisely what you were up to. In your imagination, they oohed and aahed, made comments, asked questions and were impressed by the cogency of your answers . . . They adopted your outlook and your point of view, marvelling at the ease with which you handled your un-familiar reality. (Yes: oddly enough, whereas expatriates make a more radical break with their families than impatriates, they often remain inwardly more dependent on them – soliciting their approval, fantasizing about their envy, counting on their support.)

The truth of the matter – a hard one, as truths so often turn out to be – is that you've been all but absent from their minds. Your loved ones don't spend their time trying to picture you in your new life – what a silly idea! They picture nothing at all. They don't know, so they don't care. Their minds are filled to brimming with the details of their own lives. If they think of you at all, it's only sporadically and ephemerally, like a dotted line. The exception to this rule, if you're lucky, is your parents. Parents don't usually grow entirely indifferent to their children. Your place in their hearts, though it may have grown vague, is large and permanent; it can be neither usurped nor abolished. The rule, however, is nature's tragic propensity to abhor a vacuum. Your departure did *not* leave a gaping hole back there. The lives of your loved ones are (as the French say) full as an egg.

Yes. That's the way it is. No one's amazed by what you've been up to. For all these years, you've been performing those exhausting acrobatics not to a distant gallery, but to an empty house.

In a puff of smoke, your inner witness vanishes – abruptly and irreversibly. You find yourself alone.

The Mask . . .

A person who decides, voluntarily, as an adult, unconstrained by outside circumstances, to leave her native land and adopt a hitherto unfamiliar language and culture, has to face the fact that for the rest of her life she will be involved in *theatre, imitation, make-believe.*

Naturally, you can be more or less intent on getting rid of the traits that betray your status as a foreigner. (It should be clear that I am *not* talking about the problems of "integration" encountered by poor people who immigrate to wealthy countries.) I know any number of Americans who've been living in France as long or longer than I have, but have remained faithful to their accents, blue-jeans and hamburgers, and been wholeheartedly accepted by their French entourage along with these *bizarreries*.

The fact is that you don't become aware of your own cultural values until they enter into conflict with those of a different country. I never felt particularly "Puritanical" in Alberta or New England, but on my first trips to Italy and the Riviera I was shocked by the Mediterranean way of life. It took me a while to learn to appreciate the specific beauty of *farniente*[*]; the late trains, inefficient post offices and endless aperitifs drove me up the wall. Everywhere I looked, in the very air I breathed – sun, figs, fish, soft winds, sand, music, sea – it seemed to me that there was *too much pleasure!* Pleasure without struggle, pleasure without sacrifice – "undeserved" pleasure! Thus it was that, over the years, I gradually came to acknowledge the Puritan in me.

In the theatre of exile, any number of things can "give you away" as a foreigner: your physical appearance, the way you move, eat, dress, think and laugh. Consciously or not, you observe the prevailing codes, adapt to them and gradually begin to censor the gestures and postures which are inappropriate in your new context . . . The biggest hurdle, obviously,

---

[*]An Italian term whose literal meaning is "doing nothing" and all of whose translations into English are negatively connotated: the idle life, lounging around . . .

if you're serious about your wish to become part of a foreign country, is the language.

Learning your mother tongue also entailed imitation, of course, only you weren't aware of it. You had nothing better to do! Babies never pronounce their first *goo-goos, Ma-mas,* and *Ba-bas* with an accent – they get the sounds right at once. By a process of trial and error, superfluous phonemes are shelved, vocabulary is enriched, grammar and syntax are acquired – and once learned, all these things can never be unlearned; they are cast in the bronze of "first experiences."

For foreigners, it's a whole different kettle of fish! They arrive in their new country loaded down with two or three decades' worth of neuronal baggage. Ruts have been dug, habits hardened, synapses practised, memories frozen, and the tongue has lost its gift for improvisation – hence, the mind is condemned to conscious imitation.

The results can be quite convincing – the imitation can sound almost exactly like the real thing – it all depends on how good an actor you are. Yes, some foreigners manage to "pass," a bit like the quadroons or octeroons or whatever hideous term was invented for those American blacks who took bitter pride in "passing" for white. All things being equal, women are generally better at linguistic camouflage than men (provided, of course, they're allowed to take a stab at it – not if they happen to be Turkish women sequestered in their German homes by their equally Turkish husbands). Women are born actresses. They know all about adaptation; it's part of their identity as women.

Foreigners, willy-nilly, learn to imitate. They usually find it daunting at first but they keep trying, their mastery of the adopted tongue improves and at last the day comes when they speak it fluently . . . No matter how lengthy and arduous their efforts, however, a little something almost always gives them away. The faintest trace, just a *soupçon* (good word for it) of an accent. Or . . . well . . . a modulation, an odd turn of phrase, a confusion of genres, an all-but-imperceptible mistake in the matching of verb tenses . . . That's all it takes. The French are on the look-out. They're finicky, persnickety and nit-pick-ing where their language is concerned . . . The mask slips . . . and it's too late! They've glimpsed the *real you* behind the mask and now there's no way out: Excuse me, did you say *UNE peignoire? UN baignoire? LA diapason? LE guérison???* Did I hear you correctly? Well, I'll be – you're an ALIEN, aren't you?! You come from another country and you're trying to pass your-self off as French . . . Ah, well, you can't pull the wool over *our* eyes, we've found you out, you're not a real francophone . . . "What are you? German? English? Swedish?" (Oh, I do the same thing, I admit it – the minute I detect an accent in someone's voice, I do exactly the same thing, whereas I know they've endured the same hurtful, boring, idiotic interrogation a thousand times and must be as sick of it as I am: "Are you German? No? Hungarian? Chilean?" *Which country?* as they say in India.)

Not only that, but the minute you give them the information they're after, it crystallizes in their brains and becomes your most salient feature, the thing that best describes and defines you. From now on they will think of you as *the* Russian, *the* New Zealander, *the* Malian, *the* Vietnamese or whatever – a serious magazine recently referred to film director Agnieska Holland as France's "token Pole"; another commenced a review of one of my novels with the sentence, *"Elle est morose, notre Canadienne"* (Our Canadian is in a sullen mood) – whereas back home, of course, your nationality was virtually non-existent, as invisible and inaudible as the air you breathed!

"No, Canadian," I say, blushing furiously, caught *in flagrenta dilectio* of foreignness.

"Really? Why don't you have a Quebec accent?"

"Because I'm English Canadian, and most of my French teachers were from France."

" I see."

"When I'm in Quebec, I do take on the Quebec accent, though."

"Really? How peculiar!"

It isn't peculiar, though. It's only natural.

I'm trying to get into your good graces, you see, regardless of who you are . . . I do my best to speak *like* you in order to be able to speak *with* you (by now I'm on the verge of tears) . . . Since the name of the game is imitation in any case, I see no reason why I should hang on to my Parisian accent in Montreal, rather than adapting my pronunciation to that of my dear compatriots.

In France, I need to think twice before I slip an English word into my conversation – will it make me sound snobbish or handicapped? It all depends on the person I'm talking to. The same word, the same phrase will elicit a blank stare from one friend, an annoyed frown from another, and a broad, know-ing grin from a third.

In Quebec, on the other hand (contrary to received wisdom on the subject), conversations are often peppered with English expressions, employed with a delightful sense of irony. The point is to make sure that their use is *intentional* rather than *insidious*. What militant francophones resent is having no choice in the matter – being forced to absorb English words and expressions as they emanate, pollution-like, from the all-powerful anglophone continent around them.

So in Paris I speak Parisian, and in Quebec, Québecois . . . What about in the Berry region? No.

I have to draw the line somewhere. I make no attempt to imitate the *patois* spoken by my peasant neighbours in that part of central France to which we retreat regularly during school vacations – I should feel I were making fun of them. I do, however, adapt my vocabulary to what I assume to be theirs. I try to avoid words that might seem too abstract, too intellectual, too Parisian, too Canadian, too feminist, too bookish . . . and use only . . . er . . . concrete words, is that it? Oh, the hell with it. I can always keep my mouth shut for the space of an evening. I often do. It doesn't kill me.

Whereas there's a widespread irrational prejudice against people with an accent, my own (equally irrational) prejudice is in their favour. The minute I detect foreign intonations, my interest and empathy are quickened. Even if I have no direct contact with the person in question – I may simply be walking through a park or sitting in a restaurant – my ears prick up when I hear her accent and, studying them unobtrusively, I try to imagine the other, faraway side of her life. When you think about it, there's a whole novel behind the voice of a Haitian in Montreal, a German in Paris, a Laotian in Chicago . . . "Ah," I say to myself. "That person is split in two. She's got *a story.*" Because if you know two languages, you also know two cultures – and the unsettling effects of

going back and forth between them – and the relativization of each by the other. For this reason, it
often seems to me that people with accents are more
"civilized" (by which I mean subtler and less arro-
gant) than monolingual impatriates.

Even if the foreigner is someone I know well, my
husband, for example, we can be in the middle of a
conversation – and if he suddenly picks up the
phone and starts talking in a language that's opaque
to me, I am moved. Why? In a sense, *foreignness is a
metaphor for the respect every individual owes every
other individual.* All of us are dual, at the least. All of
us are complex and multi-layered, filled with secret
memories – why do we so often ignore or pretend to
forget this fact? Even within the *same* language,
communication is a miracle. (Xenophobia proceeds,
conversely, by grinding down asperities and blend-
ing over differences among members of a group,
insisting on the reassuring sameness among them,
the better to exclude members of another group.)

People who run off at the mouth – garrulous
chatty windy gassy gushy people, those who use five
words where one would suffice – never cease to
astonish me, be they proletarians or professors. Even
now, after all these years, I can become excruciating-
ly self-conscious when required to speak French in
public. The more formal and intimidating the circumstances, the more liable my tongue is to slip,

causing me to say one word instead of another or to commit unforgivable grammatical errors. Whence, most likely, my preference for the written word. On the page, at least, I can correct my mistakes, insert a word here, delete one there . . . On the page, moreover, my accent is inaudible.

The use of a foreign tongue discourages not only loquacity but pedantry; it prevents you from taking yourself too seriously. In my case, at least, the fact that I'm perpetually aware of "playing" at being a francophone has given me a healthy distance from all my other roles in life, including those of writer and mother. The minute I start yelling at my children, for instance, my accent worsens and my vocabulary shrinks – this makes them burst out laughing and I can no longer make my rage credible; I have no choice but to calm down and laugh.

. . . So where's the real you? Huh? Let's say you decide to rip away the mask – what kind of face will be revealed? The problem is that when a human face has spent a number of years beneath a mask, deprived of light and oxygen, it changes. Not only does it age, as all faces do, but it tends to get a bit pallid, flaccid, puffy . . .

You go "home" and people can't believe their ears. *What?* You call that your *mother tongue?* Have you seen the state it's in? I don't believe it! *You've got an accent!* You keep slipping French words into your speech! This is ridiculous! Stop putting on airs! You're just trying to impress us with your prestigious Parisianism! Forget it! We won't be taken in! 'Fess up, you're an Anglosaxophone like the rest of us . . . Come on, talk normally! How dare you make mistakes? How dare you cast around for the right word? You've got all the words you need, you drank them down with your mother's milk, how dare you act as if you'd forgotten them? Talk straight, for Chrissake, talk English!!!!

Sure, yes, all right, I'd be happy to oblige . . . only . . . *which* English would you care to hear?

Just as I can pick and choose among various types of French, I now have all sorts of Englishes at my disposal.

The English spoken in my hometown of Calgary has an odd ring to it in New England, where most of my family now lives. Well, I can imitate the Boston accent, if you prefer . . . if it will make you happy . . . Or the Bronx accent . . . How about New Orleans? Just tell me what suits you and I'll try to give you satisfaction.

I'm also a master of pedagogical English – that simplified, exaggeratedly articulated version of the tongue which I taught to civil servants at the Finance Ministry in Paris for a number of years. No one speaks that language in real life, but I learned to speak it and can revive it at the drop of a hat – when foreigners ask me for directions in Manhattan, for instance.

You adapt. You do your best. You go berserk.

I recall how disturbed I was upon hearing the voice of Sylvia Plath on tape a number of years ago, in a BBC interview recorded shortly before she committed suicide. She'd been living in London for three years, and her voice oscillated within a single sentence, sometimes within a single word, between the intellectual, aristocratic British accent she was in the process of acquiring, with its crisp *t*s and narrow vowels, and the rounder, thicker twang of her native Massachusetts.

Plath's undecidedness made it painful for me to listen to her. I remember thinking, at the time, that her English was a bit like a loose woman walking down the street with half her face made up and the other half naked, normal, untouched. But now, to my dismay, my own voice has turned into that same loose woman. When I read excerpts from my books out loud to an English-speaking audience, I distinctly hear a British accent in my voice. Now why on earth would I speak with a *British* accent? It beats me. It defeats me. I don't even have Plath's excuse – I've never lived in England! In fact, I don't much *like* the British accent: to my Canadian ears, it connotes monarchy and haughtiness . . . Could it be that, even in my mother tongue, I can accept myself only as a "foreigner"?

Decidedly, the more I think about these things, the more at sea I feel.

. . . And the Pen

Foreigners, we were saying, are people who *adapt*. And the acute awareness of language instilled in them by the perpetual need for adaptation can be conducive to writing. The acquisition of a second tongue destroys the "naturalness" of the first; from then on, nothing can be self-evident in any tongue; nothing belongs to you wholly and irrefutably; nothing will ever "go without saying" again.

This can incite you to pay an unusual amount of attention to individual words, figures of speech, *manners* of speaking. (No one carried this attention to a more transcendent degree than Marcel Proust – who wrote in his mother tongue but was almost entirely cut off from it, isolated by his illness. Proust was more than a great French writer; he was the unrivalled specialist of French idioms. With the maniacal precision of an entomologist, he inventoried the manifold ways in which French was used and abused at the turn of the twentieth century, just as Shakespeare had done for Elizabethan English.) Lexical formations and deformations, assonances and dissonances, possible and impossible translations, etymologies, *nyms* of all sorts – *syno, homo, anto . . . pseudo . . .* "When you come right down to it," as Romain Gary says, "all names are pseudonyms."

Yes – *all* forms of identity, including stylistic identity, are conventional and contrived. But (is anyone keeping score?) expatriates tend to be more aware of this than other people.

The French I use in writing has all the advantages and disadvantages of an acquired idiom. Whether I deploy slangy or sophisticated vocabulary, simple or convoluted syntax, it is something I have *learned*, and can only try to use as convincingly as I can. My earliest texts in French, which date back to the mid-seventies, are rife with puns. This was partly a sign of the times (Jacques Lacan and Hélène Cixous were then making "plays on the signifier" very fashionable) – but it also betrayed my pathological awareness of the language itself. Foreigners are far more conscious of phonetical rubbings and rhymings than are native speakers. (In 1976, for instance, I wrote a short short story called *Histoire en amibe*, "Story in the shape of an amœba." Most readers probably didn't notice that this was a take-off on *Histoire en abîme*, but I did. And at the time, I was proud of my *calembour!* Almost all my titles from this period are similarly "clever," and when I see them now it makes me want to groan.)

Style, someone once said, is a marriage of love between an individual and his or her language. But can you "marry" an adopted idiom? Can you make love with a language learned through conscious imitation? And if not, how should you go about using it? Whether I take François Rabelais, Marguerite Yourcenar or Michel Tremblay as my model, the problem remains the same – none of these French languages are mine by birthright. (It would be grotesque *for me* to use exclamations like "Parbleu!" or "Tabarnak!" in a written text.) Camus and Sartre could get away with the faintly archaic *"je ne veux point,"* or *"il ne me plaît guère,"* but my own pen refuses to produce such turns of phrase. It even balks at using the simple past, a grammatical tense that somehow seems too refined for a gal from the Prairies – though my brain learned the intricacies of its conjugation decades ago.

Beckett was similarly sensitive to these issues, and I've always felt that critics paid insufficient attention to the influence of bilingualism on his style. The fact that he was an *anglophone* writer of French made him, among other things, an intrepid and screamingly funny explorer of commonplaces. In a foreign tongue, no places are common; all are exotic. "Can of worms" was a cliché until I learned *panier de crabes* (basket of crabs); these different ways of designating a messy situation became interesting to me simply *because* they were different. Bilingualism is an unending source of intellectual stimulation. Had Beckett not learned French, it would probably never have occurred to him to turn the expression *savoir-vivre* into *savoir-crever* (knowing how to die), or to complain of being "condemned to life." "The slut has yet to menstruate capable of whelping me,"* he declared in *The Unnameable*, and his entire oeuvre is a rejection of the gregarity implied by the existence of language *per se.* "I'll fix their gibberish for them," he promised . . . and he more than kept his promise.

Who am I, in French? I really don't know – a bit of everything, perhaps. When I meet with high school students, they often express surprise at the way I abruptly shift, in my novels, from the "elevated" to

---

*"Elle n'est pas encore réglée, la garce qui me déconnera!" The passage is much funnier in the original French, where both "réglée" and "déconner" have double meanings.

the "colloquial" style. Why do you do that? they ask. And I have to admit that I have no idea. Probably because I *like* doing it . . . and because it's easier for me (as a foreigner) than for them (as native speakers) to transgress literary norms and expectations. The French language is a beautiful, powerful queen. Many people who consider themselves writers are in fact nothing but lackeys in the service of this *grande dame* – they hustle and bustle around her, smoothing her hair, praising her finery, polishing her jewels, and letting her do all the talking. There's no stopping her once she gets started; you can't get a word in edgewise.

I commence a new sentence in my brain and at once it bifurcates, trifurcates – should I write "Am I seeking," "Do I seek," "Might I be seeking," or none of the above? Perhaps "Do I aim"? All right. Do I aim, then, to strip away all the stylistic accoutrements of French and achieve a sort of "degree zero," to borrow the famous expression coined by Roland Barthes? I don't think so . . . I did study under Barthes's ægis for a couple of years, however, and he definitely contributed to my extreme (not to say hyper) sensitivity to language; he taught me to be wary of (not to say allergic to) "readymade" expressions, and it is to him that I owe my penchant for parentheses, colons, semicolons, ellipses . . . and overlong sentences; I both appreciate and resent this influence.

In Barthes's seminars, as in his books, the afore-mentioned "queen" was systematically deposed, decapitated and dismembered (though Barthes himself gradually developed a highly mannered literary style). Rather than blindly putting their trust in the intrinsic wealth of the French language, his students and disciples made it their job to mistrust it because of the coded concepts for which it was the vehicle. Throughout the 1970s, French literary theory was still in thrall to the "Age of Suspicion" brilliantly analyzed by Nathalie Sarraute in the post-war years. ("Bury syntax, comrades – it stinks!" wrote Bernard Noël in 1975, for instance; or again: "No more stories – into the slop-pail!") The verb *to write*, insisted Barthes, should be intransitive. Down with the functionalization of writing, down with edifying messages; long live pure textuality, where form and content are as inseparable as oil and vinegar in a good salad dressing. Many students, overawed by the loftiness of this mission, made the verb *to write* so intransitive that it no longer dared smudge paper. If they moved away from the "zero degree," they feared they might fall into a "style" – thereby betraying their attachment to the bourgeois values they were so intent upon denouncing.

The important thing at the time, for us *Barthésiens,* was to prove that we were clever, lucid and theory savvy. We were so well trained at spotting the "myths" and political assumptions hidden behind every statement, and so blithely convinced of the absence of *any* connection between language and the world – that the credulousness required of novelists was beyond our reach. Barthes himself had dreams of writing a novel, but was brought up short by the first obstacle he encountered – namely, the difficulty of inventing proper names for his characters and then *believing* in them. Could anyone be so gullible as to fool himself that way? Like the proverbial centipede, who can't figure out which leg to start with, Barthes was paralyzed by his own need to understand how novels worked; therefore he had no choice but to renounce novel writing. Yes, whatever we say, writing fiction requires – no, *is* – an act of faith.

Not by chance did I make the leap in 1980 – daring to embark upon fiction-writing at last, just a few short months after the death of Roland Barthes. My first efforts at fiction still tried to be savvy; they gave away their own tricks and discouraged readers from believing too naively in their plots and characters . . . This is probably one of the reasons for which, some ten years later, I decided to return to writing in English. I was starved for theoretical innocence. I longed to write long, free, wild, gorgeous sentences that explored all the registers of emotion, including – why not? – the pathetic. I wanted to tell stories whole-heartedly, fervently, passionately – and to *believe* in them, without dreading the derisive comments of the theoreticians. The latter – a bit like Virginia Woolf's "Angel of the Hearth" – had begun not only to shackle my imagination but to get on my nerves.

And what did I discover? Well (ah, there's a nice, laid-back, American opening to a sentence for you) – to my dismay, I discovered that I was faced with the same stylistic dilemma in English as in French. I'd turned my back on my mother tongue for too long, and it no longer recognized me as its daughter. The whole gamut of styles was available to me – I was free to imitate the aristocratic accents of Henry James or to mimic the crude, violent monosyllables of Thomas Sanchez – but no melody came "naturally" to my lips. At this late date, I could scarcely attempt to take my place as literary representative of Alberta (besides, that seat was occupied, and no one was exactly begging me to sit in it)!

The problem, of course, is that languages are not only languages. They're also worldviews – and therefore, to some extent, untranslatable . . . And in a way, if you have more than one worldview, you really *have* none.

I'm not complaining, don't get me wrong; I kept at it as best I could and things eventually fell into place; I now have a readership on both sides of the Atlantic. (To my surprise, in fact, the books I per-

ceived as "French" often appealed to Canadian readers and, conversely, my cowboys-and-Indians novel
sold much better in France – never underestimate
the power of exoticism!) I still feel a bit dizzy when,
having translated one of my own books, whether
from French into English or the other way around, I
suddenly realize *I could never have written that in the
other language!**

And what if I had a *third* language at my disposal – Chinese, for instance? Would this give me a
third imagination, a third literary style, a third set of
dreams? Rilke in German and Rilke in French: two
different poets. Or Tsvetaeva, in Russian and in
French. If Beckett had opted for Serbo-Croatian,
would he have written *Endgame* and *Happy Days*?
What sorts of tales would Conrad have spun, had he
not abandoned his native Polish? Why did Kundera
lose his sense of humour when he started writing in
French? *Und so weiter* . . . *Who are we,* in other
words, if we don't have the same ideas, the same fan-
tasies, the same existential outlooks or even the same
opinions in one language as in another?

Oh dear. I feel a bit lost again.

It's disorientating, you see what I mean?

Which way is up?

---

*I definitely feel this way right now, as I go about translating
Nord perdu, three years after writing it in French.

False Bilingualism

There are bilinguals and bilinguals. The true and the false.

True bilinguals are those who, for geographical, historical, political or even biographical reasons (the children of diplomats), learn to master two languages in early childhood and can move back and forth between them smoothly and effortlessly. The two may play asymmetrical roles in their minds – they may feel vague resentment towards one (the language of the State or the former colonial power, the language imposed on them at school or in the workplace) – and deep attachment towards the other (the family parlance, with its connotations of intimacy and physicality, often disassociated from writing). Still, despite these possible asymmetries, their linguistic performance in both languages is non-problematic.

False bilinguals (the category to which I belong) are a whole 'nother ballgame. I don't know how the brain of a true bilingual functions, but I can try to describe what it's like to have the brain of a false one.

When monolinguals perceive a familiar object, its name automatically leaps to mind. In my case, the name that leaps depends on the language I happen to be thinking in. Sometimes one of the words comes to me when it's the other I need. Sometimes both pop up, simultaneously or in quick succession. But sometimes the process gets bogged down, clogged up, blocked off, and I could tear my hair out by the handful. If I remember *bagpipes*, I forget *cornemuse* and vice versa; the same goes for *chèvrefeuille* and *honeysuckle*. There are words that stubbornly refuse to make the trip from my brain cells to my lips, no matter what language I require them in – words I never find when I need them. *Indigent*, for example. Or *empirical*. Then there are what the French call "false friends" – words which look and sound the same in both languages but have different meanings; these tend to cancel each other out. I end up avoiding them completely, just to make sure I won't mix them up. *Eventuellement. Eventually.*

Harassed. Harassé. Ostensiblement. Ostensibly.

As a general rule, in French, I find it hard to remember seldom-used words that designate a precise object rather than a genre. I can find the equivalent of *tool* but not *wrench, utensil* but not *spatula, fish* but not *bass, bird* but not *woodpecker, flower* but not *nasturtium, tree* but not *ash.* Other French words are stored in my brain in phonetic groups: there's a whole drawer reserved for nouns ending in *eau,* for instance. If I speak without thinking, it's as if I were grabbing words out of the drawer at random, and I'm quite capable of saying *tableau* (painting) or *rideau* (curtain) instead of *plateau* (tray).

The other day, coming across the word *perron* (doorstep) on a printed page, I suddenly drew a blank. It was a strange feeling. I've pronounced this word any number of times over the years, both silently and aloud, I've even included it in my writings on occasion, and I haven't particularly neglected it in recent years . . . How dare it just "go out" like that in my brain – even momentarily – when my back was turned? But there it was; the word meant nothing to me. It *refused* to mean anything. A bit like Louis Wolfson in *The Schizo and Languages,*[*] I

---

[*] In *Le Schizo et les langues,* the New York author Louis Wolfson describes his violent allergy to his mother tongue and his ingenious efforts to "cancel out" English words by "hearing" each of their separate syllables as a word from another language.

felt my mind flash through a number of hypotheses, from the Italian *però* (however) to the Spanish *perro* (dog); even the colourful Evita Peron was briefly summoned to my assistance – but no, there was nothing for it; these suggestions were swiftly rejected and for a few seconds I sat there with an empty brain.

Things are not likely to improve with the passage of time – on the contrary. And since I'm married to a Bulgarian-born francophone, we're sometimes filled with dread at the perspective of a quasi-autistic communal old age. At first our acquired language will desert us bit by bit and our sentences will be studded with blanks: "Could you get me the . . . ? You know, the thing that's hanging from the . . . in the . . . ??!" (We're struck by the highly specific place our memory reserves for *nouns*. Nouns are what you lose first in a foreign tongue – just as, in your mother tongue, you lose your hold on proper names. My husband, who has some notion of linguistics, explains the singular nature of nouns by the fact that *designation* and *predication* are two different types of activities. Nouns, he says, are the anchors connecting us to the ocean floor of reality; without them, we would float on the surface, bobbing here and there on waves of verbs and adjectives.) Eventually, with French totally erased from our memories, we shall sit in our rocking-chairs from dawn to dusk, nattering incomprehensibly in our respective mother tongues.

Some monolinguals are naively convinced that you can get from one language to another with a good dictionary and a grammar textbook. How wrong they are! As a matter of fact, these tools are virtually useless for everyday communication. The next time you take public transportation, imagine that there's a foreigner at your side, and that it's your job to translate to them, word for word, everything you hear in the course of your trip. Listen carefully to what the other passengers are muttering in their beards . . . "How's tricks?" "Come over for a bite?" "None o' that fuckin' shit." "Gotta blow." "Let's catch a few z's." "He hit the ceiling." "Where're ya comin' from?"

It's only when these myriad opaque expressions finally become transparent that you can say you really *know* a language. And even then, you'll *never* know it the way native speakers do. It still happens – not every day, but more often than I care to admit – that I stumble upon a French word I could swear I've never seen before . . . whereas my children are perfectly familiar with it. How is this *possible?* A child's memory is like a sponge (knowledge accumulates within it), whereas an adult's is like a sieve (knowledge runs through it).

Merely *knowing* a word, moreover, doesn't necessarily make you capable of using it.

We had our dear monolingual friends A. and S.

over for dinner the other night. When I said there were any number of French words and expressions which I, as a foreigner, felt unable to use in conversation, they were incredulous.

"Like what?" they asked.

"Well . . . the simple past tense, for example."

"Oh, that doesn't count. Only members of the Académie française use the simple past tense in oral speech! It's grotesque. What else?"

"Well, uh . . . certain expressions. *Il me les gonfle*, for example. (He's a pain in the ass.) I can't say that. Or anglicisms, like *news* (print media), *challenge* (challenge), *look* (image, personal appearance). Or abbreviations like *perso* (personal)."

"Oh, that doesn't count, it's really more a matter of generation and social milieu than of language . . ."

"Well then, *le cas échéant* (should the case arise), especially pronounced with the *liaison, le cazéchéant*. I can't say that."

"Oh, that doesn't count, that's technical, a legal expression . . ."

And so on and so forth. They didn't believe me! They didn't understand! Whereas they, of course, do the same thing all the time. And so do you. All of us make decisions about which words and expressions to include and exclude from our active vocabulary. Only expatriates do so, however, after conscious, lengthy, obsessional, not to say paranoid reflection.

For false bilinguals like myself, nothing is more painful than to have to "process" messages in both languages at once. I experience this virtually as a physical combat in my brain – and the mother tongue invariably comes out on top, whether I like it or not. A few months ago, I had lunch with a francophone friend at Schwarz's, a famous Jewish deli on Saint Lawrence Boulevard in Montreal. She was confiding to me in a low voice about the problems of her first marriage – but halfway through the meal, four hearty hefty middle-aged men came in, evidently regular patrons of the restaurant; they sat down at the next table and started talking loudly in English. Despite my ardent desire to concentrate on the fragile, precious, hesitant, trembling, tearful story of my Québecois friend's marital disaster, all I could hear now were anglophone inanities. "Hey, waiter! Could you bring me the head of the bread? Just tell the cook it's for me, he knows I'm crazy about it. The head's the best part, you know. Never eat anything but the head of the bread!" At the end of the meal, I realized to my despair that I would *never* know the details of my friend's marriage; it was not the sort of story that you can ask someone to repeat.

For decades now, I've been dreaming, thinking, making love, writing, fantasizing and weeping in French, in English, and sometimes in a monstrous mixture of the two. For all that, the two languages are neither superimposed nor interchangeable in my mind. Like most false bilinguals, I often have the feeling that they "sleep apart" in my brain. Far from being comfortably settled in face to face or back to back or side by side, they are distinct and hierarchized: first English then French in my life, first French then English in my writing. The words say it well: your native or "mother" tongue, the one you acquired in earliest childhood, enfolds and envelops you so that *you* belong to *it*, whereas with the "adopted" tongue, it's the other way around – you're the one who needs to mother it, master it, and make *it* belong to *you*.

Every false bilingual no doubt has his or her specific map of lexical asymmetry. For my part, I prefer French to English in intellectual conversations, interviews, colloquia – linguistic situations which call upon concepts and categories learned during my adult life. But when I feel like letting off steam, freaking out, swearing, singing, yelling, surfing on the pure pleasure of verbal delirium, I do so in English. In other words, all my French is apparently located in my left brain – the hyper-rational, structuring hemisphere which governs my right hand – whereas my mother tongue, which I absorbed at the same time as I learned about sphincter control and the interiorization of taboos, is more "bilateral" (distributed over both hemispheres). Thus, my right brain – the more holistic, artistic, emotive part – is entirely anglophone.

A month or so ago, following a public debate on the subject of exile in Ajaccio (Corsica), a Scotswoman drew me aside. "I married a Corsican," she told me, "and I've been living here for more than twenty years. I speak French fluently and from morning to night, with no difficulty . . . But . . . how shall I put it . . . somehow, even after all this time, the French language doesn't *touch* me, and this drives me to despair." The woman indeed seemed on the verge of tears. "When I hear *bracken, leaves, fog*, I can see the hues of ochre and brown, I can smell the scents of autumn, feel the humidity . . . whereas the same words in French – *fougère, feuilles, brouillard* – leave me cold. I don't feel a thing."

I sympathized. It was because this woman, like myself, had had a non-French childhood. She had not absorbed along with her mother's milk (as all French people have, including my own children) the lullabies, jokes, whispered secrets, nonsense rhymes, multiplication tables and administrative departments of France, to say nothing of the *Fables* of La Fontaine or the *Confessions* of Jean-Jacques Rousseau.

"And that's not all," continued this Scotswoman-turned-Corsican or this Corsican-born-in-Scotland. "In English I'm squeamish about swearwords. Even when I'm beside myself with rage, I scarcely dare murmur the word *God* – whereas in French the worst obscenities cross my lips with ease. I can say *putain, salope, enculé de ta mère*, and not even blush."

Here again, I sympathized intensely. The subject of my Master's thesis in Semiology, written under Barthes's supervision, had been linguistic taboo – a prickly topic, to be sure, but an endlessly fascinating one. French swearwords, blasphemies and insults were probably more accessible to me as an object of scientific study than they would have been to a native speaker, because I didn't react to them emotionally. *Foutre* (fuck) was neither more nor less shocking to me than *fastueux* (lavish); I'd needed to look both of them up in the dictionary.

Yes, I think this must be the most important thing: the French language in general (and not only its forbidden lexicon) was to me less emotion-fraught, and therefore less dangerous, than my mother tongue. It was cold, and I approached it coldly. It was a smooth, homogeneous, neutral substance, with no personal associations whatsoever. At least at first, the fact that I was blithely ignorant of the historical, psychological and social backdrop against which I was writing gave me a heady sense of freedom in my work.

This advantage, however, was not without its

drawbacks. In a way, I was almost *too* free in French. Like the Scotswoman, I was untouched by the language. It did not talk to me, sing to me, rock me, slap me, shock me, scare me shitless. It was indifferent to me. In a word, it was not my mother.

It so happens that I became fluent in French at almost exactly the same time as I discovered the harpsichord (1971). And that, two years later, when I abandoned my mother tongue, I also abandoned the piano. A strange and secret paradigm has come to form and deform my thinking about these things for the past quarter of a century. I see *English and the piano* as motherly instruments: emotional, romantic, manipulative, sentimental and crude. In both, variations in dynamics are emphasized, exaggerated, imposed, flagrantly and unavoidably expressed. *French and the harpsichord*, on the other hand, are neutral, intellectual instruments. They require control, restraint and delicate mastery; their expressivity is infinitely more subtle, discreet and refined. Speaking French or playing the harpsichord, in other words, there are never any violent surprises or explosions.

What I was running away from when I turned my back on English and the piano seems quite clear.

Nature and Nurture and Nature

For years now, in both my writing and teaching, I've been speaking out against the Sartrian model of self-engendering – the "all-culture" stance that declares: *I am a rational, sovereign, free and autonomous adult, entirely the product of my own will.* Sartre expressed nothing but disgust for nature, heredity and reproduction; he could not stomach connections to others which were imposed, predetermined, rooted in biological necessity. Of course, Sartre was not alone in this; the anti-kitsch tribe includes Kundera, Beckett, Kafka and many more: down with mothers! Down with family love, togetherness, smooch smooch fart fart the twittering of little birds and the sweet fragrance of forget-me-nots wafting over green pastures all the way to the horizon. Long live freedom, struggle and heroicism; long live Orestes who murders his mother and lays the foundations thereby for Western philosophy, long live depression and Prozac, the tragic conscience of the solitary man faced with the dizzying meaninglessness of the swirling cosmos.

Man – or rather, what this philosophical construct calls "man" – is a transcendent subject who chooses and invents himself. A bit like a weed endowed with hands, he pulls himself up by the roots to escape from the muck of determinism. His goal is to transmit knowledge, not genes – "to shape souls, not bodies," as Simone de Beauvoir put it, in an effort to explain her preference for teaching over motherhood (as though mothers had no part whatsoever in the shaping of souls!). The fact is, however, that most adult humans become parents – and that all of them *have* parents, and that, whether we like it or not, to *be* or to *have* a parent is to be connected to other people by love and hatred, chromosomes and history.

The anti-kitsch tribe calls these non-chosen bonds "contingencies," and describes them as ropes which hamper our freedom. "In the language of the smallest European people," writes Kundera in *Testaments Betrayed*, "the word family is *fjölskylda;* the etymology is eloquent: *skylda* means obligation, and *fjöl* means multiple. Thus, the family is a multiple obligation. Icelanders dispose of a single word with which to say family connections: *fjölskyldubönd,* namely, the bonds of multiple obligations."

Of course, the illusion of self-engendering, solitude and sovereignty is far easier to maintain if one does not have a father. Because of World War I, an entire generation of French thinkers – including Sartre, Camus, Barthes, Bataille and others – grew up fatherless and thus, to some extent, weightless, free and indeterminate, without a superego. Not being obliged to drag along the heavy baggage of the past, they could entertain the pleasant fancy of living in a perpetual present, reborn each day and destined to immortality. "I never cease to create myself," writes Sartre in *The Words,* "I am the donator and the donation" – or again: "Rather than the son of a dead man, I was made to understand that I was the child of a miracle." All these men, in other words, aspired to become the sons of their own works . . .

Although, as I said, I've often spoken out against this model, I must admit that it has also been my own. When I put on my francophone mask and took up residence in a foreign culture, was I not declaring my preference for freedom and autonomy? Here, in effect, is what I was telling my friends and family back home: I can, must, and will go my own way, without your help, advice, or judgment. My plan is to invent myself, day by day and year by year. You see? Now I've become a part of this other world, a world over which you have no control, within which you have no authority, and whose language is impenetrable to you. Not only that, but I have married someone from yet another country, yet another culture, and you're helpless to intervene. I am travelling and changing, turning into someone else! My body is being shaped by foods and my mind by books different from yours; I'm moving away from you, creating myself, and there's nothing you can do about it. Stay in touch if you feel like it – but know that, whatever happens, you've lost me. Every time we meet, I shall be slightly more unrecognizable.

Unknowable.

And then . . .

Twenty-five years later, brushing my hair in front of the mirror, what should I see between my eyebrows but . . . two small vertical lines! The lines of Granny Huston!

Our grandmother used to frown so often, or at least so my brother and I surmised to each other in whispers behind her back, that the trace of her discontent was indelibly imprinted on her flesh, visible even when she smiled. Hmmm. Have *I*, too, become a constant frowner, then? As sour, stern and strict as Granny Huston? I don't *think* so . . . But then, perhaps *she* was not as stern and strict as I recall? It's the old story of the chicken and the egg: did my grandmother have lines between her eyebrows because she was stern, or did I think she was stern because of the lines? Is it possible that these stigmata are being passed down by the Huston chromosomes, independently of the psychological outlook of the face that wears them? What a frightening thought!

When you hit forty, nature starts catching up with you.

At twenty, with a modicum of discipline and luck, you can invent your own appearance. You're smooth and svelte, silky and shimmery, you make original choices in clothing and hairstyles . . . "I'm my own woman now," you think; "I don't owe anything to anyone!"

Twenty years later, you're forced to think again. Inexorably and irrefutably, the very atavistic defects from which you recoiled as a child start rising to the surface. The lines that made your granny's face seem stern, the greyish rings beneath your father's eyes, your great-aunt's facial hair, your mother's moles, *her* mother's bunions, and so on and so forth.

Ah! And if only nature would be content with reclaiming your body! But no – it wants your soul as well!

As an intransigent young French revolutionary with eyes of fire, you spat upon Christian attitudes of charity, mercy and forgiveness; now they begin to regain ground inside of you.

Having spent decades in a nation famous for its irony, sincerity (which for the longest time you thought of as naïve, not to say ridiculous) suddenly appeals to you.

Having admired the exquisite verbal lace of writers like Pascal Quignard, you now hanker after plain old wonderful stories *à la* Jim Harrison.

Having enjoyed the complicated etiquette of three glasses and six forks, you yearn for greater simplicity in table manners: "Pass the ketchup!"

Having appreciated the circumlocutions of French *politesse* (Ah, you are hoping to seduce Monsieur de Nemours by pretending not to know who he is, whereas, although it is true that you never set eyes on him until today, you are every bit as much aware of his identity as he is of yours – am I correct, Madame de Clèves?), you begin to miss the brutal frankness of American conversation – "How much do you make?"

The music of Rameau and Couperin suddenly sounds pale and sickly to your ears, and you're amazed to find yourself putting on records by Johnny Cash or Nat King Cole.

You reconsider all the things you once rejected, weighing their pros and cons, acknowledging their validity.

What about Sartre, Kundera, Kafka, Beckett and the whole anti-pipsqueak crowd? Did they really notice nothing, as they stood in front of their mirrors and watched themselves age? Sons and fathers of their own works, did they manage all their lives long to hang on to the illusion that they were books and nothing else? Sartre's autobiography (significantly entitled *The Words* and divided into two sections, "Reading" and "Writing") ends when he reaches the age of ten. We have no way of knowing whether, as he wrote this book in his late fifties, he had a dawning awareness of something like a specific moral, psychological or physiological *inheritance* . . .

Whether we like it or not, we bear a physical and spiritual resemblance to our parents, grandparents, ancestors, the social milieu that shaped us and the country in which we were born . . . These factors determine us, not totally but partially. People truly *are* Jewish or black, male or female, whore or thief, Canadian or French – *these things exist,* not only in the eyes of others but *in reality,* and they have certain consequences. Freedom is part of human identity, but so are constraints.

In the final analysis, *absolute freedom exists only in our desires,* not in our reality. Both are crucially important. It's just as dangerous – and in my opinion just as reprehensible – to neglect the limitations of the real world as it is to renounce the vertiginous flights of our imagination.

The Misery of the Foreigner

At the end of September 1959, while my parents were getting divorced in Western Canada, the woman who was soon to become my stepmother took me with her to visit her parents in a tiny town in Germany by the name of Immerath. The trip was interminable and excruciating. Three days and three nights on the train from Western to Eastern Canada, another day from Montreal down to New York, followed by a full week on the boat – a week of uninterrupted hurricanes (or so it seemed to me), in the course of which I could swallow nothing without bringing it up at once. Then, more long hours of train travel, from Rotterdam to Cologne, and still more hours by car, from Cologne to Mönchen-

Gladbach to Immerath, where at long last we reached our destination . . .

On the evening of our arrival, in the village school where my new grandfather taught and where my new mother's family lived, my new grandmother had prepared a feast for us – huge platters of disquieting cold cuts (tongue, liver pâté, head cheese), beet and cabbage salads, marinated eggs, black bread and hard, miasmic cheeses . . . Everything on the table was foreign to me, to say nothing of the people seated around it or the language in which they spoke . . . Foreign – *and, therefore, threatening*. I don't know how else to put it.

Did tears come to my eyes? I don't know. What I do know is that I kept my head down throughout the meal and touched nothing on my plate. And Wilma, my new mother's lovely younger sister, saw that I was in a bad way. Towards the end of the meal, she rose abruptly, slipped on her coat and left the house. About an hour later – it was pitch dark by this time and the dinner guests had long since dispersed – she returned with a triumphant smile on her face and . . . a box of Kellogg's Corn Flakes in her hand. She'd driven some thirty miles to buy it.

I think this must have been the most delicious meal of my life – a banal bowlful of the all-American breakfast cereal, wolfed down at nine o'clock in the evening in a foreign kitchen, in a foreign house, in a foreign country, on the cusp of a new life in which I was going to have to survive without my mother. I'm eternally grateful to Wilma. The young German woman with hazelnut eyes and a crooked smile has since turned into an eccentric old lady who lives amidst eighty-three cats and their excrements . . . But on that long-ago evening, she realized that a little Canadian girl was in desperate need of something *familiar*, and I'll never forget it.

Ah! people exclaim. You're so lucky – you get to travel! You've been to India, Japan, Mexico, Timbuctoo . . . How I envy you – it must be marvellous!

Sure. Visiting foreign countries is often interesting. But it's also unsettling. Anxiety-provoking. Disorientating. How do we manage to forget it? Every time I cross a border, it comes back to me in a flash – oh yes, *this* is how it is. Again. The misery of the foreigner. I'm now past the age, even in Italy, even in Spain, where men ogle me and follow me around in the street, brush up against me and whisper filthy nothings into my ears; moreover, I've acquired a modicum of confidence and *savoir-faire* . . . Nonetheless, foreign countries continue to disturb me.

The minute I find myself on the far side of the border – the language. A blank wall. Impenetrable human beings. They laugh, and you've got no idea what they're laughing at. They wave their hands in the air and shout at each other, and you can't even guess what all the excitement is about. It's really rather nightmarish, when you think about it. Even if you physically resemble the natives, which of course is not always the case, they single you out at once. All you need to do is pronounce a single word, and they know you're not from here. "*I . . .*" No. Not *I.* Come up with something else. You're gagged. You mumble, stumble, fumble, you don't know where to begin. You fish out your tourist guide and, flipping through the pages of "Common Expressions," manage to squeeze out a few syllables; people snicker and look at you askance; you feel like a dunce.

The same thing is true in Paris, if you happen not to be fluent in French. People who don't speak a word of *any* foreign language – and who, for this reason, consider French to be a "natural," "given," self-evident mode of expression – are especially likely to be baffled by your lamentable efforts to find your way around in their verbal universe. You yourself may be fluent in seven or eight *other* languages; no matter – if you use a masculine adjective with a feminine noun, watch out! They'll put on the same air of condescension, pity and annoyance ("Come, come, surely you can do better than *that!*") as if you had shoved a forkful of mashed potatoes into your ear.

In a foreign country, you become a child again, in

the worst sense of the word. You're infantilized, reduced to *infans* – that is, to silence; deprived of the faculty of speech. Utterly helpless and handicapped. (It was clever of the English language to make muteness and stupidity converge in the word *dumb*.) All that's left to you are logistics, of which every least detail seems insurmountable. Where's the post office? How do pay phones work around here? What are all these coins for? You know *nothing, nothing!* How much should I pay for a rickshaw? Am I being ripped off? What's he laughing about? What do the headlines mean? I want my corn flakes! Mother! H-E-E-ELP!

In Poland one day, I remember approaching an elderly man in the street and asking him for directions in English. He stared at me uncomprehendingly and answered me in Polish. Naturally, I didn't understand a word; and, come to think of it, he looked rather like an idiot, his face was closed and his features obtuse, he seemed to me the very embodiment of stupidity, I was beginning to lose patience when suddenly he tried French – *French! French!* – pure, simple, sublime, transparent, *human* words! Oh, yes! How wonderful! I understand you, sir! I worship you! Thank you so much!!!

Never forget this story. Foreigners are stupid. This time the French language expresses it well, associating *étranger*, foreigner, with *étrange*, strange.

Barbarian: "foreign, strange, ignorant," says my

French dictionary. "Echoic base: *barbar*, used for the unintelligible parlance of foreigners." Anyone with whom you cannot communicate verbally is perceived as ignorant . . . *and* threatening. Romantic verbiage notwithstanding (the universal language of music, the harmony of the spheres, the instant intimacy of hearts, the beauty of body language and so forth), words continue to be unbeatable as a means of communication.

I have a dream – it's more like a daydream, really, or a fantasy. In this dream, I'm as powerful and invisible as God. I lean down over France, pick up Jean-Marie Le Pen[*] by the scruff of his neck like a little kitten, and plunk him down in the middle of a foreign country. (Hasn't he always said, "You don't understand, we *like* foreigners – in their own countries!" So let's see.)

In this country, Jean-Marie has no political power. He is exactly like you and me. Normal, naked. Well, no, dressed – but in ordinary clothes, not a uniform. He's the president of nothing at all, he represents no authority, he doesn't have the right

---

[*]Le Pen is leader of the extreme-right political party Le Front National, which has often campaigned against the presence and rights of foreigners in France. In April 2002, his popularity was still so great that he made it to the final round of the presidential elections.

to give orders, push people around or thunder into microphones. He's just a man. Rather obese and unattractive, but still – a man. Inordinately pink-skinned, I grant you – but a man, all the same. So here he is, suddenly abroad – in a city, say, somewhere in the heart of China or India or Africa, wherever, almost any country will do. All around him, the city's inhabitants are going about their business, working, playing, exchanging gossip . . . And, of course, Jean-Marie understands nothing of what's going on. I can see him standing there, overwhelmed by the misery of the foreigner, shrinking into himself and getting suddenly all shy and polite. A terrified, submissive, obsequious Le Pen, doing his best to ingratiate himself with the "natives." Where will he be able to sleep tonight? How do the hotels work here – and indeed, *are* there any hotels? Excuse me, sir . . . Er . . . sorry to bother you . . . Do you speak French? No? Er . . . *Hôtel?* I'm dead tired. Gotta get some shut-eye . . . You know, sleep! Like this – zzzzzz! And I'm starving to death. I could eat a horse . . . A horse, you understand? Whinny-whinny-whinny . . . No? Oh, please . . . aren't there any restaurants around here? Res-taur-ant?

Jean-Marie doesn't know a soul in this country. He doesn't even have an Aunt Wilma to go out and buy him a butter croissant.

That's it. That's my dream. Just like that.

The Arrogant Mosaic

Someone sent me a copy of a *Toronto Star* article dating from August 1998, shortly after France's triumph in the soccer World Cup. You may think, the article says overall, that France's enthusiasm for *Les Blues*,[*] a mixed Black-White-and-Arab team, reflects a global policy of racial tolerance and generosity. Well, you've got another think coming. "Racism is very much alive and well in France, in a disgraceful departure from the ideals of the 1789 Revolution. And it will remain so until the French

---

[*] *Sic:* An interesting chauvinistic slip – in fact the team is called "Les Bleus."

begin to emulate the Canadian model of true multicultural equality for all citizens."[*]

Exactly what "multicultural equality" might mean is not specified. The expression not being set off by quotation marks, it is apparently assumed to be common knowledge. What *is* set off in quotes, however, is the word "foreigners." Included in this category, pell-mell, are French-born children of immigrants from France's former colonies in North Africa, newly arrived refugees without papers, Kanaks (from New Caledonia, who are French citizens) and Jews. "There are more than four million 'foreigners' in France," states the author of the article – and, having conveniently tossed all of them into the same boiling cauldron, he goes on to paint a horrifying picture of their situation in France.

This country – Canada – which puts the word foreigners in quotes, happens to be a country made up almost exclusively of foreigners, a country in which the word has no discriminatory function because it designates virtually anyone and everyone. In 1789, at the time of the famous Revolution lauded by the *Toronto Star*, Canada was seventy-eight years short of Confederation.

Upon arriving in Canada, did we (the French, English, Irish, Swedish, German, and Armenian

---

[*]Haroon Siddiqui, "What France can learn from Canada," *Toronto Star*, 9 août 1998.

immigrants to Canada) *ask* the local populations if they agreed with our "multicultural" ideals? Having appropriated their land in order that our own cultures might thrive there, isn't it a bit caddish of us to pat ourselves on the back for not being racist?

Come one, come all! Whether you hark from Sri Lanka, the Ukraine or Saudi Arabia – the more the merrier! Look, there's plenty of land! Millions of acres at your disposal! Settle in, make yourselves at home, you're welcome to go on speaking foreign in private, provided you learn English (or *à la rigueur* French) for public life . . .

That is the origin of the Canadian mosaic. "As paradoxical as it may seem," my brother wrote in a recent letter, "the paternalistic, condescending multiculturalism of English Canada is the exact equivalent of Québecois nationalism. They're simply two different ways of maintaining a good conscience while continuing to feel superior to those you perceive as aliens."

Perhaps what I'm trying to say is this: *it's easy to be "multicultural" when you don't have a culture of your own.*

Okay. I said it. But, having said it, I've also given myself away as an emigrant, a national apostate, a traitor to the Great North. Because, deep down, I know that this vision of Canada – my vision, the one

I

sarcastically formulated just now – is false. *That* Canada is not the real Canada – rather, it is an artificial construction, shaped by public discourse for political purposes. Deep down, I know that the real Canada is a fine place to live. I know that the texture of everyday life there, as real people live it, is rich and variegated. I know that Canadians are creating world-class literature and film, theatre and dance; I know they have specifically Canadian community activities and figures of speech; I know they're profoundly attached to their neighbourhoods and gardens, churches and houses, cafés and restaurants . . . I also know that *these things add up to make a culture.*

It's because I'm so woefully ignorant of this culture – because I'm not a part of it, because I so rarely get the chance to feel it, taste it, and press it to my heart – that I can sit here, all these miles away, and peremptorily declare, "They ain't got one."

Sour grapes, in other words.

Relatively Relative

What is important? we asked ourselves above. (Yes, I know, I keep repeating myself, contradicting myself, going around in circles – but that's just the point. I'm trying to get my bearings, don't you see? It's only natural that I should be going around in circles.)

What is important? For ordinary people, the answer to this question is self-evident. What matters is what's close to me. A series of concentric circles – my family, my friends, my neighbours, my school-mates, my compatriots – with "me" at its centre. I'm touched by what touches me.

For the expatriate, once again, *nothing* is self-evident. Those to whom you feel close are far away. For the first few years, you think of them all the time and are affected by everything that happens to them. By writing letters, making phone calls, buying newspapers from back home, you do your best to reduce the gulf that has opened up between you . . .

Vicissitudes are what make your new life begin to feel less like a "trip abroad" and more like life *tout court*. As long as you keep rushing around your country of exile in a state of bedazzlement, marvelling at the novelty of everything you see, you're merely a tourist among others. This behaviour can last for weeks, months, or even years. You quit the "tourist" state when, in a foreign country, you experience new forms of despondency and distress. (One December in Paris, having just had my heart broken, I purchased a giant Suchard chocolate bar in a bakery and ate every square of it as I wandered tearfully through the freezing grey streets of the thirteenth *arrondissement*. This moment has remained engraved in my memory, and I'm sure it has contributed at least as much to making me "French" as my naturalization.)

As time goes by, your communications with "back home" become fewer and farther between. Imperceptibly, your friends from there are replaced by friends from here; now *they*'re the ones who ask you the important questions: How's that 'flu of yours? When's your boss going to get around to giving you a raise? Did you see the article in

Le Monde about . . . ? What are your plans for the weekend? Godawful weather, isn't it?

Your former friends gradually lose interest in you, and vice versa. Why go on writing to each other if you're never going to share your lives again? And then one day, perhaps, in the foreign country, you found a family of your own. The years keep slipping by. Your parents age, your siblings change jobs and/or spouses, have children, remarry, redivorce, you can't keep up with it all; that is, you register the facts, but somehow you don't *identify* with them in the way you used to; it takes a willed effort to share in their joys and sorrows . . . Here too, of course, the estrangement is mutual.

The foreigners who surrounded you when you first arrived in France have become your compatriots. Now it is *their* destiny that means the most to you, because it has become *your* destiny. For years, you've been living with these people, reading their newspapers and sending your children to their schools; little by little, you've come to understand them and identify with their reactions; you can put yourself in their shoes . . . And ultimately you realize that those shoes aren't even "theirs" anymore, they're yours. You've become French. You vote in French elections, help count French votes, take part in French social and political debates . . . The political situation of your native land, to the (limited) extent that it's ever mentioned in France, now seems "exotic" to you.

Guilt, once again. The gap between you and your country has grown so wide as to be unbridgeable. The issues which you used to see as earth-shaking have grown virtually meaningless.

So who are you?

Relativization. Forced. Vertiginous.

And when you go "back," when you spend a few weeks at "home" (that is, in the place that used to be and is no longer your home but continues to act as if it were, welcoming you with open arms as if you had come "home at last"), there are almost never any references to France. Your adopted country takes up very little space in the newspapers, still less in the minds of your friends. The space it does take up is coloured by clichés (wine, wit, fashion, good food, perfume, sophistication and superficiality) – clichés which no doubt correspond to certain realities, as clichés are wont to do, but which have precious little to do with the complex warp and woof of your everyday life in France.

No one has ever heard of the conflict between Jacques Toubon and Jean Tiberi, or the Elf scandal, or the Houellebecq phenomenon, or the violence in the suburbs. No one knows about the high school student strikes, the public transport strike, the feminization of the names of professions, the thirty-five-hour workweek, this year's Beaujolais. They've heard of Depardieu, Le Pen and that's it; their perception of contemporary France ends there.

What conclusions should we draw from all this? That love is relative, family togetherness insignificant, and patriotism an arbitrary attachment?

What is important? Yes, I know, more circles. Yet I'm convinced that everything is *not* relative – or at least, only *relatively* relative. Having spent long years struggling with this question, I've finally arrived at something which vaguely resembles an answer.

What is important can be translated.

You need have no specific interlocutor in mind. Take an imaginary friend from *back there,* a sort of ideally benevolent, intelligent, curious and cultivated listener, and pull up a comfortable chair in your brain for her or him to sit down in. Now do your best, in this person's mother tongue, to explain the conflict between Toubon and Tiberi. Your listener may nod politely, but this won't deceive you – you can tell that her smiles are in fact disguised yawns; this means that your story is unimportant. Now, take the Canadian controversy between francophones and anglophones and try to make it interesting to a peasant from the Berry. Yes? It's working? Great – that means it's probably important. But if you start talking about the infighting among the various proponents of *souveraineté,* you'll lose your audience in a matter of seconds. And so on and so forth. This should help you to distinguish between Cyclone Mitch and a tempest in a teacup.

A good book, unlike a blockbuster bestseller, is almost always translatable. So are truly good jokes. The tomfoolery of the *Guignols** may delight French television viewers today, but within a month or two even they will have forgotten what was so funny. Woody Allen is hilarious because his jokes appeal to Hungarian and American audiences alike.

All pain is translatable, from the toothache of a dental assistant in Idaho to natural catastrophes like the floods in China.

This seems to me an excellent criterion.

Translation can also serve as a form of *protection* in moments of distress – when, for instance, you find yourself at a "typically French" dinner party, where the name of the game is being clever at each other's expense, making fun of everyone and revealing nothing of yourself. If this game upsets you, either because you've never learned how to play it or because you *have* learned and despise yourself for doing so, all you need to do is mentally translate the conversation into your mother tongue. Ah . . . You see? You feel better right away. Your imaginary

---

*Les Guignols is a satirical puppet show broadcast nightly at prime time, which systematically derides France's political and cultural élite.

friends are every bit as shocked as you are by this gratuitous display of nastiness.

There's a hitch, though. There's always a hitch. Uh-huh. You guessed it. Real friends are far less patient, polite and available than imaginary ones. No matter how well you translate, nothing guarantees that they'll take an interest in the things you find important. Too bad . . .

You can always resort to writing.

The Three Daughters-in-Law

As was stated earlier on the subject of accents, women tend to have a more flexible conception of their identities than men. They're taught to adapt from birth onward; and they do; they get used to it. Upon getting married, they may be expected to take on not only a new name (which is already *a lot!* I mean, do you men *realize?* Think of all you invest in your patronym, both emotionally and symbolically, and try to imagine what it would feel like to change names once, twice or more in the course of your adult life!), but a new political allegiance, a new religion, nationality or language . . . Thus, women are often aware that all these facets of identity are relative rather than absolute.

Men tend to *identify* more blindly and passionately. They may be asked to kill or die for what they have been taught is *them, theirs* – their name, their honour, their country. Women know that their identities can be violated, transformed. A Sabine girl can turn into a Roman woman overnight, and her sons may later engage in mortal combat with her brothers. She knows, therefore, that the "givens" of her birth identity can be acted upon and changed.

To take my own case: notwithstanding my origins as a middle-class white anglophone, born in Alberta and theoretically destined to marry, say, a professor at the University of Calgary, it so happens that I've had three very different mothers-in-law. (In French, by a strange quirk of philology, the same word – *belle-mère* – is used to designate both mothers-in-law and stepmothers!) Three more or less elderly women in whose presence I maintained a respectful silence – and who, because I was living with their sons, welcomed me into their homes and treated me with the kindness and hospitality reserved for close members of the family.

The first, a gruff, overweight lady whose sole vocation in life was that of a Jewish mother, lived in a cushy, well-appointed home in the West Bronx, New York. The second, a retired schoolteacher who had been active all her life in the Socialist Party, lived in a grim little allotment on the outskirts of the city of Bourges in central France. The third, a frail and self-effacing former librarian, lived in a rustic wood-en house in the hills on the fringe of Sofia, Bulgaria. In turn, I enthused about their *gefiltefisch,* their *boudin blanc* and their *guvetch.* Nodding, laughing and sighing at the appropriate moments, I listened to their respective stories about "my man" as a little boy.

If I could be all of these things (and I could, and in our day and age it's not all that unusual), to what identity may I still lay claim? The answer is *not* "any and all." I took up residence neither in Bulgaria nor in the United States but in France. I'm French because I partake fully of the life of the French people.

I do have a small advantage over the natives, however – I know that "to be French" is only one of many possible identities, the result of a series of geo-graphical and historical accidents. Thus, I am aware of my good fortune – and aware, too, of all that remains to be done.

Memory Gaps

At least one thing is sacred, you keep telling yourself. There's at least one part of my being that can be neither invaded nor altered, and of which I can never be dispossessed – my memory.

(Everyone has heard the incredible tales of men who preserved their sanity throughout years of captivity by forcing themselves to remember all the names of their classmates in grade school . . . or all the piano sonatas they had committed to memory in their teens . . . Practised over a period of weeks and months to fight off boredom and despair, these exercises in concentration can indeed produce spectacular results.)

So we think of memory as inviolable. Thick as

thieves, my memory and I. Inseparable, till death do us part. "*You can't take that away from me.*"

Unfortunately, this, too, is false. Yet another reassuring illusion bites the dust. The truth is that our memories, like our tastes, ideas and political opinions, are shaped by our everyday lives. They change, shift, meld, mix, dissolve and disappear.

In 1995, during my summer retreat in the Berry, I received a letter from Susan P., my "best friend" between the ages of fifteen and eighteen, before and after high school graduation. I hadn't heard from her in ages – and suddenly, having somehow found my address, here she was pouring out the story of her adult life to me on thirty-five foolscap pages – her studies, her marriage, her political activism, her work as a sculptor, her children . . . After having lived for a number of years on the West Coast and in the Southern United States, she'd just moved back to her mother's house in the backwoods of New Hampshire, where we'd first met.

Leaning over the large wooden chest in the entrance to our country house, with sunlight streaming through the windows, I read Susan's letter surrounded by the voices of my (French) children, the twittering of (French) birds and the lowing of (French) cows; the sentences looped across the yellow pages in all directions, often culminating in decorative flourishes and doodles ("She hasn't changed . . ."), and my eyes blurred with tears.

It so happened that I was planning to visit New England the following month, so I wrote back promising to look her up. And thus it was that we came together on a beautiful September's day, in a bookstore not far from where we'd parted more than twenty years earlier. Let me pass quickly over the shock of the encounter itself – our unrecognizable bodies, the hypocritical exclamations ("You haven't changed!"), our incredulous poring over of snapshots of our respective children . . . Sitting in one of the local yuppie no-smoking bars, we downed beer after beer, laughing and weeping, basking together in the exquisite pain of nostalgia . . . A few beers down the line, though, it became clear that something was "off." There was a feeling of discomfort . . . What was wrong?

Every time I said, "Do you remember . . ." Susan said yes. But when *she* attempted to revive a memory, I often drew a blank. There was one adventure in particular of which I hadn't the slightest recollection . . .

No, there was nothing for it – I rummaged through my memory from basement to attic (would I have put it in the "1970" file, the "runaway" file or the "sexual initiation" file?), opening all the cupboards and chests of drawers, even flipping back rugs in the event that I might have swept the memory under them in a fit of spring cleaning – not a trace. "I'm sorry, I don't remember." And Susan paled. "How can you not *remember?*" she exclaimed, over and over again. "I don't believe you! That story is part of my life – my life with *you!* I've told it to everyone. It's one of my founding memories, and you're in it. You *can't* have forgotten it. I mean, who am I, if you don't remember that?"

Guilt, yet again.

Yet the explanation was simple. These memories had died of inanition. You've got to pay visits to your memories from time to time. You've got to feed them, take them out and air them, show them around, tell them to other people or to yourself. If you don't, they waste away.

For a quarter of a century, nothing in my French life had revived those specific images. No landscape, individual or event had sparked off the electric signal which might have summoned or awakened them. And so, little by little, and without my noticing it, they had faded into nothingness. In my memory (that is, in the mental image I have of my own life history), I did not run away with Susan P. during a school outing to the Green Mountains in 1970. We did not hitch a ride together . . . We were not picked up by two drunken bastards armed with guns . . . None of this occurred. I can identify with the "Nancy" who experienced those things, but no more nor less than I can identify with a character in a novel. I cannot recognize her as being "myself."

(Immediately after my return to France, I sent Susan the manuscript of *Thrice September* – a novel that evokes some of my own memories of those years. I haven't heard from her since.)

Long before Alzheimer's sets in, our memory is a construction, a tale filled with gaps, a book with ripped-out pages. This is true of everyone, but (ah, by now we must be pulling into the lead) expatriates grow aware of it more rapidly than others.

We forget the non-essentials . . . *and* the essentials. Piddling details and crucial insights. The banal and the intolerable. (Like the unique and incomparable nature of childhood, this flagrant imperfection of memory is an awareness which exiles share with psychoanalysts.)

Conversely, were I to return to live in America for the final decades of my life, the details of my French existence would gradually sink into oblivion. And in the year 2025 or so, a friend from the Berry might come to visit me in New York, we'd have a drink together in the coffee shop across from the Metropolitan Museum, and she'd say, "Remember that awful storm of 1999, when Jacques's roof was blown off?" Staring at her in perplexity, I'd knit my brows (between which, of course, Granny Huston's lines would now be etched more deeply), and ask, "Er . . . what are you talking about? Who is Jacques?" *

---

*I can't resist pointing out that this essay was written in the fall of 1998. I had no way of knowing that France would indeed be swept by a storm of unprecedented violence in 1999, and that one of our neighbours – Claude, not Jacques – would have his roof blown off.

Other Selves I

Today I stayed home.

When it stopped raining, I didn't go out to admire the dance of cloud and sunlight on the surface of the Seine, the gasp of pink, rippling, wind-whipped waves.

For the umpteenth time, I did not take my son to visit the Paris sewers.

Nor did I go hiking in the Rocky Mountains with my daughter.

I did not drop in to see my mother in Montreal, in her lovely house nestled against the mountain, with its bay windows looking out over the cluster of downtown skyscrapers and all the way out to the giant bridges that span the Saint Lawrence.

Nor did I take a jaunt to New Hampshire to see my father, still busy refurbishing his old house on the edge of the river. The river will soon freeze over, and I shall not go skating on it.

I did not go careening madly, joyfully, down the wide sidewalks of Amsterdam Avenue in Manhattan, whirling in the wind amidst the garbage and dead leaves.

I did not have a big, hearty breakfast in the coffee shop of Sainte-Rose-du-Nord, on the Saguenay River, with my dear Québecois friend Jean Morisset. Oh, how fragile and friable I felt, that morning last October, as I listened to Jean strike up a conversation with the attractive owner of the place, Indian blood in the veins of both and the French language an instantaneous bond between them. The incredible intimacy afforded them by the use of the familiar *tu,* the way words from the vernacular *joual* vocabulary moved back and forth between them like caresses, and the scenes they both remembered from their childhood in that part of the province, the river and the fjord, the big American ships, the impoverished, over-large, under-educated families, the endless freezing winters and the dishes their mothers used to make, vegetables cooked to a pulp and fricasseed potatoes in *sauce au poche* (egg sauce) – the *tourtière* (meat pie) made only at Christmastime – a *culture,* that was it, this woman and Jean shared a *culture,* and as they sat there exchanging the signals of this culture in low voices I felt sullen and jealous, realizing that there wasn't a person in the world (apart from my brother, who lives more than three thousand miles away from me) with whom I could have this reassuring sense of being recognized: *"You're one of us, you belong here, we'll stick together through thick and thin."*

No, I stayed home.

And yet, in one way or another – by way of telephone conversations, letters, photographs, or simply memories – all of these worlds were part of my day today.

The various strata of our lives coexist within our minds – and we somehow manage, at least until Alzheimer's sets in, not to mix them up. For me, the word *train* carries with it echoes of freight-trains from my Alberta childhood, passenger trains in Germany, trains read about in novels or seen in films, the death camp trains exuding retrospective dread, and a train which I once heard in the gorges of the Allier River in Central France, its whistle filling me with a mysterious, piercing nostalgia as it faded into the blackness of the night.

I suddenly see with crystal clarity that my vocation as a novelist dates back to my childhood – when, to reassure myself and perhaps even to survive, I had to learn to convincingly conjure up the love of the person who is usually the very symbol of proximity and presence – but who, in my case, was far away and permanently inaccessible. And it's quite possible that all the permutations I've put myself through, all the disparate roles I've embraced, then rejected – the three daughters-in-law, the university professor, the nude model, the feminist intellectual – have been my own way of asking (a bit like Romain Gary, albeit for different reasons), "Like this, Mummy?"

Our freedom to go elsewhere and be other people in our minds – to espouse religious, national, sexual and political identities other than our own – is truly mind-boggling. Reading and writing novels reminds of how important this freedom is – the quintessence, indeed, of all human freedoms.

Life is an unending flow of infinitely diverse impressions. We receive, classify and organize these impressions, responding to them with a flexibility which far surpasses that of the most sophisticated computer. We know how to be a thousand different people in turn, and we name the sum of these people "I." We use the same word to designate the self who is a friend, a parent, a reader, a hiker; the distracted self; the self who stares in awe at the beauty of a Gothic cathedral; the self who drinks, laughs, smokes, or watches TV; the narcissistic self; the contemplative self; the vulgar, alert and droopy self. These myriad selves dart to and fro like schools of tiny, slippery, glittering fish, and as it is impossible to catch them in the net of language, we generally content ourselves with summing up the extravagant flux of our lives in a few pat phrases: "Yeah, had a great summer"; "Doing fine, just fine."

Were we to open ourselves utterly to the flux, the multiplicity, our own infinite capacity for reception, we should go mad. In order to preserve our sanity, we make ourselves short-sighted and amnesic. We strive to keep our experience within certain fixed limits. We stake out the same territory day after day, calling it "my life" and defining "myself," tautologically, as the person who stakes it out. We decide, for instance, that "my life" will be that of a literary critic, a professor of mathematics in the Paris suburbs, a rap singer, a prostitute, a Buddhist monk hidden away in a monastery . . .

Literature allows us to cross the borders – as imaginary as they are indispensable – which circumscribe and define our selves. Reading, we allow other people to enter us – and if we make room for them so willingly, it's because we know them already. The novel celebrates our miraculous capacity to recognize others in ourselves, and ourselves in others.

Of all the literary genres, the novel is the *genre humain.*

Other Selves II

Normal people proceed from one stage of their lives to the next in much the same way as snakes moult. Of course, they evolve and change; they commonly refer to the successive "phases" of their lives . . . Still, they tend to see their *identity* – that is, their sense of who they are, of what they do and why they do it – as a constant.

Not so for expatriates.

Nothing but uncertainty, nausea, and – again – dizziness, at the idea that you could have been somewhere else, you might have done something else, you should have met someone else . . . and that the life you actually do lead is, well, singularly lacking in reality. Conviction. Coherency. Consistency.

Where am I dear Lord who am I where do I come from – and especially, why? *Hier ist kein Warum*, isn't that right? It was for *no reason at all* that You decided I should be born in Calgary, the daughter of those two individuals, in that particular language and social milieu! I'm not complaining, don't get me wrong, I think I was dealt a fairly good hand at the game's outset, that's not the problem, it's just that . . . I mean . . . the whole thing is so damn *arbitrary.* I'm right, aren't I?

Well, it's a bit unsettling. (At the same time, I'm aware that were it not for the milieu into which I was born and the education I received, I wouldn't even be able to ask You this sort of question. A woman living under the Taliban regime in Kabul would never dare to pester You like this.)

Every expatriate has the conviction – deeply rooted in her subconscious and regularly rejected as preposterous by her intellect – that a part of herself, or, rather, *another self,* has never stopped living *back there.* (In literature, this illogical conviction was immortalized by Henry James in "The Jolly Corner.")

Yes, I know – *and yet . . .*

I know I've been living in Paris for all these years, and yet it's simply not *possible* that, at the same time, I'm not walking in the cool, bright transparency of an October morning in New York, under an incomparably blue sky, down those hard efficient streets of glinting metal and glass, amidst the rushing well-dressed crowd, between the high granite walls near Grand Central Station, or near the Empire State Building where I once worked as a temporary secretary (only on the fifty-eighth floor), or near the Juilliard School of Music where I practised piano after work every day for a year, or near Central Park, across from the Museum of Natural History, where I transcribed hundreds of hours of tape recordings for two eccentric intellectuals, one a sociologist and the other a psychoanalyst.

(I'm not talking about a visit or a trip; I'm talking about habits. Daily routines that have vanished. Few mental experiences are stranger than that of mentally reliving, gesture by gesture, a daily routine that is no more.)

No, I mean, seriously. *How is this possible?* You mean to tell me that *on no real level* am I still stuck in that cramped apartment on the ground floor of a dilapidated building on 196th Street in the Bronx, where for two years I battled roaches and depression while listening to the complaints of the fat Jewish ladies as they paused to rest on my doorstep on their way home from shopping, talking in loud voices just beyond the door, so that as I sat hunched at the living-room table, trying to force my brain to follow the intricate abstract reasonings of Freud and Aristotle,

I was continually pulled back to their *kvetching* about bunions, ungrateful sons and *gefiltefisch?*

No? I don't live there anymore? Not *at all?* Really? And what about the "Blue Bar" of the Algonquin Hotel, with its good jazz, gin fizzes and salted nuts, and the grey-templed, debonair, dignified men who engaged in earnest conversation around low tables, while slinky slips of girls in backless black dresses with carefully made-up faces and seductive smiles stood at the bar . . . I was one of those girls back then . . . You mean to tell me that all this keeps going on day after day, year after year, and *I'm not part of it anymore?* I'll never be part of it again? That's *incredible . . .*

January 1997: I was having lunch in a coffee shop in New Delhi when a young Western woman caught my eye. She had the shaven head, ascetic features and magenta robes of a Buddhist monk – but, incongruously, she was engrossed in reading a novel . . . Intrigued, I contorted my body into a position that allowed me to read the book's title: it was *The Unbearable Lightness of Being* by Milan Kundera . . . And when the woman rose to leave, I saw that beneath her monk's gowns she was wearing . . . Air-Max Nikes.

Ah yes. The unbearable lightness. Only one life. Not two. Not thirty-six.

Yet I insist – all these years after my departure from Alberta, there's a *me* who continues to live back there. I like her a lot. She's a spunky dame – a Calgarian proud of her Irish stock, a true Western gal with a noisy, gutsy, almost mannish laugh, a ruddy face, a body that's taller and heftier than my own, weighing about 145 pounds, she has a generous stride, broad gestures and hips, which means that giving birth to her four or five children was a breeze, men have come and gone in her life, some of them husbands, others not, but all her children have remained close by, growing up with her and worshipping her, bringing their friends over to meet her, then their lovers, then their own spouses and/or children, yes it's quite possible that this woman is already a grandma because she got off to an early start, the first baby came when she was eighteen and the others followed bing bang bong, now her hair is turning grey and she doesn't give a hoot, she isn't fussy about her appearance but she enjoys wearing carmine lipstick and heavy Mexican silver-and-turquoise earrings, she's anything but a highbrow, she started working as soon as she finished high school, and before you could say *boo* she was running her own real estate company, this was back in the 1970s, the oil boom years, she made a pile of money and what she likes to do with money is spend it, hand it out, some would say squander it, she does so with gusto, as she does everything else, whether it's weeding her vegetable garden, or making coffee over a campfire in the Rocky Mountains or giving herself body and soul to the body and soul of the man of the moment or whipping up batches of muffins for breakfast or barbecuing steaks for dinner – she dishes out life all around her, ruffling hair or whacking bottoms according to the needs of the moment, she doesn't mind a little vice and a little violence every now and then, it does her good, she hollers when she feels like it, cusses like a sailor, plays poker with a vengeance and drinks her beer straight from the bottle, in fact one of her front teeth is chipped because she once tried to drink beer and jitterbug at the same time, she loves to dance, when she goes out to dance halls on Saturday nights she plays the clown, plays the whore, doesn't give a hoot what people think, buys rounds of drinks for her friends, prefers the company of men to that of women because men are better laughers and drinkers than women are, they don't sit around whimpering about their problems, she despises milksoppishness, coquettery, daintiness and poltroonery, insists on looking a problem in the face and confronting it head-on and solving it herself, be it a leaky roof or a despondent child, she knows how to take the bad along with the good, knows how to ski and ride horses, values mastery and muscles, loves to cruise round the city in an old pick-up truck – driving fast, dangerously fast, with the radio turned up full blast, singing at the top of her lungs . . .

Yes . . . that's the part that hurts most of all . . . That this woman sings the songs which I myself have lost or forgotten, songs which are fading and unravelling in my memory, or songs I never learned but should have learned, songs I wish I'd had the chance to learn – her voice rumbles in her abdomen and vibrates in her chest and comes bursting from her throat, the words are hilarious or poignant or downright silly . . . And meanwhile I sit here in the country of harpsichords and castles, sequestered in silence from morning to night, endlessly shuffling words around on a grey screen . . .

The Buddhists are right – and so is Kundera – this lightness of being is perfectly unbearable. Who can accept the idea of having only one life?